This book belongs to:

....

Pierre
THE MAZE DETECTIVE

THE MYSTERY OF THE EMPIRE MAZE TOWER

Hiro Kamigaki & IC4DESIGN

Laurence King

HOW TO PLAY

1 First, find the **START** ....>
Follow the maze until you find Mr X
who will be next to the **GOAL** ....>

2 On each maze, solve **EXTRA**
CHALLENGES from *Mr X* and
respond to written requests from
other characters.

3 Try to **FIND** gold stars, red trophies,
green and red treasure chests, and
other **HIDDEN OBJECTS** in each of
the mazes.

4 If the course is **BLOCKED**, find an
alternative route. You can walk past
a person or animal on a path only if
there is room to pass them. If there is
more than one possible course,
choose the **SHORTEST**.
You can climb up and down steps and
ladders as long as there is a path on
to them. You can also cross flat objects
such as carpets.

5 **PUZZLE PAGES** have smaller mazes
and additional challenges that must be
solved before you can move on to the
next page, so pay careful attention to
the instructions on each one!

PICTURE THE SCENE...

It is morning. A ship steams over the still, sleepy ocean towards a city of soaring skyscrapers on the horizon.

This is New Maze City, where buildings compete to be the tallest. Standing in their midst, shimmering in the morning sun, rises the tallest of them all: Empire Maze Tower. Most of the ship's passengers are heading there for the Christmas holidays. Pierre, however, has a different purpose. He has a feeling that something big is going to happen. Pierre has a special talent for looking into the distance and seeing what lies ahead.

Why? Because he is the solver of mazes . . .

THE MAZE DETECTIVE!

Pierre
The Maze Detective

Carmen
Pierre's friend

Mazey
The Maze Dog

Lord Candy
Owner of
Empire Maze Tower

Mr X
The Phantom Thief

On Deck

All the passengers are relaxing on board. Carmen has created a maze for her dog, Mazey, to solve. Pierre is talking to other famous detectives about their greatest cases. Suddenly, Lord Candy, millionaire owner of Empire Maze Tower, announces: "You have all been invited here for a reason. I have received a letter from Mr X the Phantom Thief. He plans to steal the Maze Cube from the top of my tower. If he succeeds, New Maze City will be plunged into darkness. Catch him, or Christmas will be ruined!"

Mysterious Letter from Mr X

My dear Lord Candy,
Tonight, at exactly midnight, I
plan to steal your precious Maze
Cube from Empire Maze Tower. You
and your little detective friends
will never catch me! I am always
watching you, but can you see me?

From X

REQUEST FROM THE CHEF

Someone has taken
the melon I need for
my delicious Fruity
Ice Cream recipe.
Can you help me find it?

Hidden Items

☆ 1 GOLD STAR

🏆 1 RED TROPHY

📦 1 RED TREASURE CHEST

The New Maze Times   VOL.1

Maze detectives from around the world meet on luxury ocean liner

A number of famous detectives are heading to New Maze City with
Lord Candy to help him in a perilous quest. Have you spotted them all?

Pierre The Maze Detective

Carmen Pierre's friend

Mazey The Maze Dog

Lord Candy Owner of Empire Maze Tower

Mazelock Maze Sleuth

Maze Explorer

Maze Master

Maze Sergeant

Maze Cowboy

Maze Solver

The Ocean Liner

Hundreds of boats and planes are speeding towards New Maze City for the holidays. Pierre and Carmen must get there ahead of the crowds, but what's the best way ashore?

Quick! Head down the steps, round the pool, and past the giant fish on deck, then up again.

"Woof!" Why is Mazey barking? It's Mr X! He's at the lifeboats! What now? Into another lifeboat, and after him!

Mr X's Pirate Challenge

My dear Pierre,
We meet again! I have hidden 10 pirate flags marked with an X, one for each of the people chasing me. You and your detective friends can't leave the ship until you have taken them all down.

From X

Hidden Items

⭐ 3 GOLD STARS
🏆 3 RED TROPHIES
📦 1 RED TREASURE CHEST

Captain's Request

I'm too busy to feed my pet elephant. Could you take an apple from me and give it to him?

I'm sure he's relaxing on board somewhere . . .

SIGHTSEEING

Be sure not to miss:

• a game of minigolf
• 5 couples dancing
• a movie being made
• a red life boat
• a pink dolphin

A Crowded Port

The port is packed with ships and tugs, yachts, and rowing boats. There must be a way through to the dock. Heave! Heave! Row left, past the *Mamie Smith*, then round to the right. Watch out for floating logs!

On dry land there's not a moment to lose. Find your way to the footbridge, cross over, and look for the tram stop. Who's that waving as the green tram jolts away? Mr X! We'll just have to catch the next one . . .

Mr X's Henchmen Challenge

You didn't think I'd come alone, did you? My gang are all waiting for you, in their red-and-white striped shirts and red socks. Spot the five in vertical stripes before they capture you!

From X

Hidden Items

⭐ 4 GOLD STARS

🏆 3 RED TROPHIES

🧰 2 GREEN TREASURE CHESTS

POLICE REQUEST

A group called the A Gang have been smuggling wild animals into New Maze City. They have been spotted driving four black cars marked with a "A." Please find them and inform the police.

Missing Fish

Our delivery of fish has gone missing from Marine House. If you see the five blue barrels, please return them before the fish go rotten and start to stink!

New Maze City

Honk! Honk! Traffic jams make your tram late. It's already lunchtime on Christmas Eve and New Maze City is bustling with shoppers. In the crowds you keep catching glimpses of Mr X's purple cloak. Follow him into Labyrinth Gardens and then down past the toy shop. He loves toys and games! Watch out for horses as you cross the road and hurry back to the gardens.

There he is again, disappearing into the grand entrance of Empire Maze Tower . . .

TOWER

GOAL

POISON SNAKE CHOCOLATE

LEGENDARY TREASURE

HAMLETS 202 FOR TOYS AND 200 GAMES

HAMLETS HAMLETS HAMLETS HAMLETS HAMLETS

HAMLETS

WARLOCK BROS. DOWN TOWN THEATRE

THE GREAT LABYRINTH

Mr X's Christmas Challenge

My dear Pierre,
I feel like we are old friends now.
Knowing you can't resist a challenge,
I have hidden your Christmas present
to slow you down. An "X" marks the gift.
It's good to have a surprise from time
to time, isn't it?

From X

Hidden Items

☆ 4 GOLD STARS

♙ 4 RED TROPHIES

📦 3 GREEN TREASURE CHESTS

Appeal from Parents

Our little boy went
missing while we
were shopping. He's
wearing a red sweater
just like ours. Please
help us find him in
time for Christmas!

Groom's Wedding Invitation

Today is my wedding day.
I am waiting in front of
Empire Maze Tower but
my bride has not arrived.
If you bring her to me,
you can join in
our celebrations.

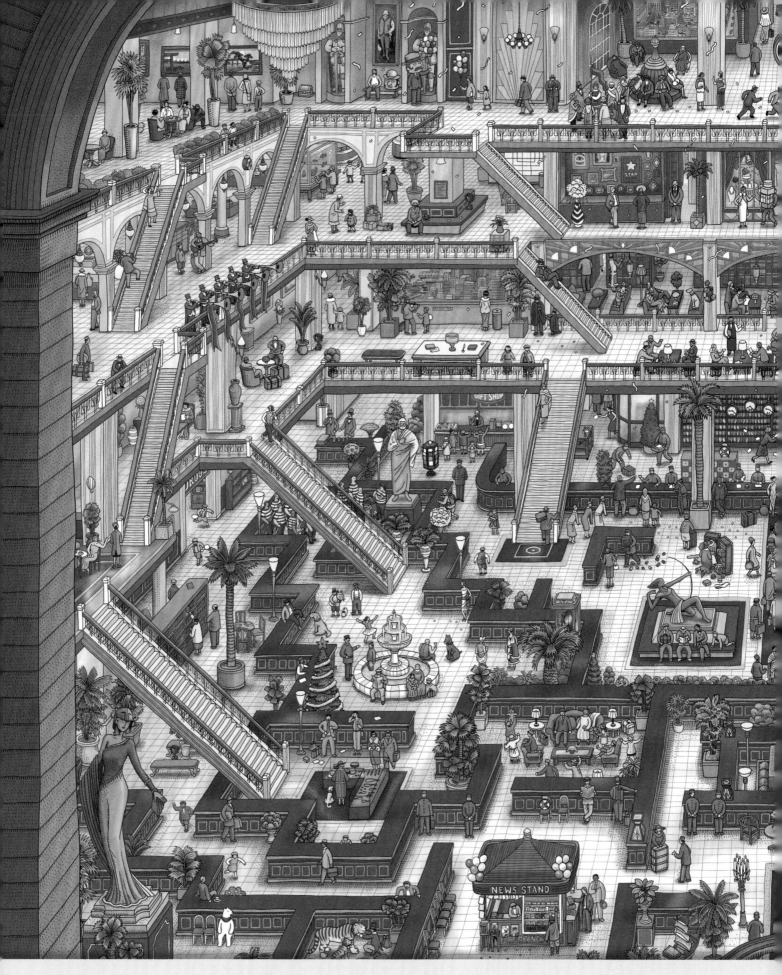

Main Lobby

Wow! The first thing you see inside Empire Maze Tower is a huge lobby filled with statues, staircases, shops, and people. A porter greets you.

"Has Mr X checked in?" asks Pierre.

"Yes sir! He was heading towards the Candy Store. There's a bit of a crowd at the main desk, but you can drop your bags and head up the stairs and if you're quick you might catch him!" There's the main desk in the middle with all the bustling porters, but how do you get to it?!

BOURGEOIS

GOAL

PERFUME

START

Mr X's Alarming Challenge

I have hidden five giant alarm clocks around the Main Lobby. They are all set to go off at once, spreading panic through the hotel. Can you find them in time? You have just three minutes!

From X

Hidden Items

☆ 5 GOLD STARS

🏆 5 RED TROPHIES

📦 2 GREEN TREASURE CHESTS

REQUEST FROM THE RECEPTIONIST

We are so busy today. Could you lend us a hand?

First, catch the dog that is running off with someone's hat.

After that, please find the father and child wearing red cloaks and guide them to the exit.

Invitation

All guests are invited to see the tower's new statue being unveiled. But the famous sculptor is nowhere to be found. He has curly blond hair and a fantastic pink suit. Have you seen him?

Candy Store Puzzle

All the detectives gather in the Candy Store. It is filled with all the candies, lollipops, and toys you could ever want. The shopkeeper looks very nervous.

"I have a message from Mr X," he says. "He has hidden five chocolate bars in a maze on the floor. If you can solve this maze and find three rocking horses hidden on my shelves, I am to give you free tickets to the Amusement Park."

While the other detectives argue, you set about solving the puzzle!

Hidden Items

⭐ 3 GOLD STARS

♟ 2 RED TROPHIES

🟫 1 GREEN TREASURE CHEST

🧸 1 TEDDY DRESSED IN BLUE

CARMEN'S CHRISTMAS LIST

- a blue Eiffel Tower
- a toy Ferris wheel
- a purple Santa
- a pink teddy bear

Request from the Girl in the Yellow Dress

I'd like a candy from the jar with the heart on it, to the left of the letter "N." It's very high up. Could you please help me reach it?

The Amusement Park

Upstairs from the Candy Store, doors open on to a huge terrace. There's a rush of cold air and the sound of screams and laughter.

It's an amusement park, high above the rooftops! There's a giant Ferris wheel, merry-go-rounds and carousels, even a zoo. Hand in your ticket and jump on the rollercoaster. Mazey is waiting for you at the top. And look, up there! It's Mr X, climbing even higher, up to the hotel rooms . . .

Hidden Items

- ☆ 6 GOLD STARS
- 🏆 4 RED TROPHIES
- 📦 3 GREEN TREASURE CHESTS

★ ★ ★ ★ ★

Free Ride

Find these five red stars and win a ticket for a ride on the Ferris wheel!

ESCAPED GORILLA

A giant gorilla has escaped from the hotel zoo. He's going wild! Can you find a bunch of bananas and feed them to him?

The New Maze Times
VOL.2

Tightrope walkers attempt new world record

Tightrope walkers from all over the world have arrived in New Maze City. They are attempting a new world record for walking on the highest wire between skyscrapers. Will they do it?

What if they fall?

Can you spot one of them between buildings?

Guest Rooms

The door opens into a hotel full of staircases and wondrous bedrooms where guests from around the world can enjoy different activities for a personalized stay. Which way? Up, up, and up, through room after room towards the towering Christmas tree with the red star.

"Mr X is up in the Library!" someone shouts. "But you have to climb all the way down before you can go up again!"

LIBRARY

GOAL

HERE

Hidden Items

☆ 5 GOLD STARS

♟ 4 RED TROPHIES

🗃 3 RED TREASURE CHESTS

Mr X's Monkey Challenge

My dear detectives,
You are getting too close! So, I've let
five monkeys loose in the hotel. Can you
find them? You have five minutes before
they start tearing up the rooms.

From X

GETTING WARM

Message from Hotel Porter

A guest has ordered afternoon tea, but I've forgotten the room number. She's in the Mermaid Room.

Any ideas where I can find her?

Let's peek into a few rooms.

In which room:

• has a big present been delivered?

• can you see a fun-looking slide?

• is there a mysterious crystal ball?

• is someone hiding in the bathtub?

Library Puzzle

What has happened here? The detectives have all made it to the Library, but the place is in a terrible mess.

"Mr X gave me a message for you all!" says the hotel chef. "He has stolen the *Book of Amazing Mazes*, which shows the path to the Maze Cube. You cannot follow him until you solve the two maze puzzles he has set for you. One is hidden in the bookshelves along the edges, the other is through the books on the floor."

GOAL

Hidden Items
- ☆ 4 GOLD STARS
- ♟ 3 RED TROPHIES
- 🧰 2 RED TREASURE CHESTS
- 🎩 1 RED SILK HAT
- 🚢 1 TOY SHIP

REQUEST FROM THE CHEF

I only came here to get a recipe for Christmas pudding. Could you help me find it?

The recipe is in a yellow book next to an eye mask, near the bottom of the shelves.

NOTE FROM THE LIBRARIAN

To confuse Mr X, I tore out page 8 from the *Book of Amazing Mazes*. If you can find the page, you might get to the Maze Cube before him.

Secret Message

There is a secret message hidden in the design of the bookshelves. If you step back and stare at the shelves, can you make out the words EMPIRE, MAZE, and TOWER? Hidden within them is a book called *Monster Juice*, which will help you in your quest.

Great
Exhibition

Up the stairs from the Library is the Great Exhibition. It is filled with fantastic creatures and treasures from ancient times. This is normally a quiet place, but not today! Mr X has set free the exhibits from the Hall of Dinosaurs and Monsters. How can you get past them?

Climb up and down the ladders and run along the top of the walls. Grr! Roar! Careful not to get trampled by a four-headed beast or grabbed by a Cyclops. And don't fall into the crocodile pool!

Hidden Items
- ☆ 5 GOLD STARS
- 🏆 4 RED TROPHIES
- 🎁 3 RED TREASURE CHESTS

CHEF'S ADVICE
Find the chef and give him the *Monster Juice* book you found in the Library. He will use it to make a special drink for calming down monsters! He's wearing a red neckerchief.

Mummy's Request
The mummies from Egypt are running wild because they want their mummy! She is wearing pink bandages and hiding from all the noise. Can you find her?

The New Maze Times VOL.3

Opening of Fairy Tale Hall at Great Exhibition

A new display of objects from the world's best-loved fairy tales opens today at the Great Exhibition in Empire Maze Tower. Don't miss your chance to visit the Cinderella Room, with its beautiful pink carriage. Arrive before midnight to avoid disappointment.

START

Golden Theater

"Hurrah! Bravo!" In the Golden Theater everyone is clapping and cheering. One of the escaped monsters, a green dragon, is on stage. People think he's part of the show!

In all the commotion, Mr X is getting away. Follow him through the seats. Up the steps. Past the orchestra. There he is! Mr X is high up in the gallery, waving back at you. There's no time to lose . . . he's escaping into the darkness of the Boiler Room!

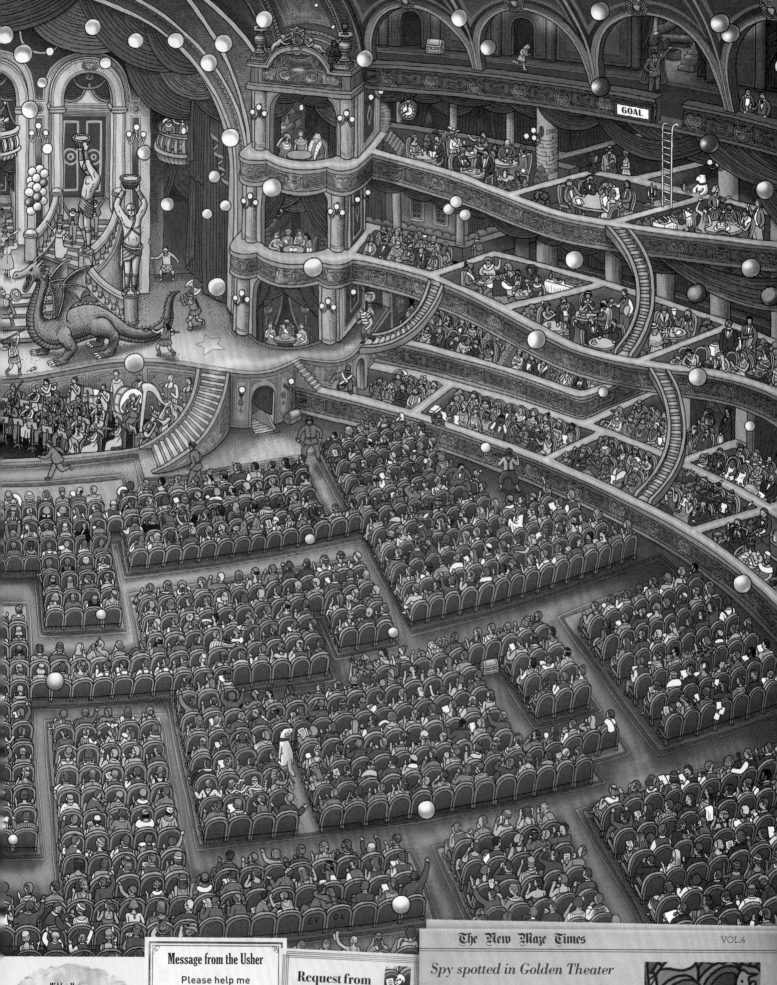

GOAL

Hidden Items

- ☆ 3 GOLD STARS
- 🏆 3 RED TROPHIES
- 🧰 4 GREEN TREASURE CHESTS

Message from the Usher

Please help me take a message to:

- a king with his daughters
- three drummers sitting near the back

Request from the Director

Oh no! The actor playing a skeleton hasn't learned his lines. I need him for the next scene, but he's hiding somewhere. Please find him and bring him to me.

The New Maze Times

VOL.4

Spy spotted in Golden Theater

The new production of *Beauty and the Beast* opened last night to rave reviews. The show is so good that a rival company has sent a spy to steal the best ideas. He is reported to be wearing a ghost costume as a disguise. Have any of our readers spotted the spy?

Boiler Room

Chug! Clang! Rattle! Listen to the roar of the Boiler Room's engines. Huge cogs grind and groan far below. Boilers rumble. Puffs of steam blast from metal chimneys. It is boiling hot. A tangle of twisting, turning pipes stretches away into the darkness.

There must be a way across. Balance on the hot pipes. Don't bump into Mr X's henchmen. Don't look down. And, whatever you do, don't fall off!

Hidden Items

☆ 3 GOLD STARS
🏆 3 RED TROPHIES
🧰 3 GREEN TREASURE CHESTS
🧰 2 BLUE TREASURE CHESTS

MAINTENANCE ORDER

Valve number 6 is not closed properly. Find the tools needed to do the job and take them there immediately.

Plea from a Henchman

Help! I'm afraid of heights—I can't move. Find the first aid kit and bring it to me, and I promise to work for you instead of the boss.

Hurry, I can't hang on forever!

Mr X's Jack-in-the-Box Challenge

Surprise! I've placed 10 jack-in-the-boxes on the pipes. If they pop up, they might make you jump. And you don't want to jump in this maze! You have five minutes to find them all.

From X

START

Observation Deck

Wow! What glitter! What sparkle! The exit pipe from the Boiler Room is a secret entrance to the Observation Deck. Did you ever see anything so beautiful?

Look through the world's biggest windows at the city lights twinkling like stars. Marvel at the fountains pouring from towering statues. Wait! It's getting late! There's no time to gaze at the views. Mr X has found the lift to the Grand Ballroom. And the maze through the swimming pools is one of the hardest yet . . .

GOAL

Hidden Items

- ☆ 6 GOLD STARS
- 🏆 3 RED TROPHIES
- 💎 4 GREEN TREASURE CHESTS

REQUEST FROM THE LIFEGUARD

Please help me find:

- a mermaid combing her hair
- someone diving
- a marriage proposal
- a clown holding a ball

BEST VIEWS IN THE CITY

The Observation Deck offers guests of Empire Maze Tower the best views in the city. Enjoy spotting the building with a maze on its roof.

Mr X's Black Paint Challenge

Dear detectives,
In five minutes, I plan to spoil everyone's fun by pouring paint into the beautiful blue water. Ha! The only way you can stop me is to discover my five cans of black paint.

PAINT CAN

From X

Grand Ballroom Puzzle

All the detectives are enjoying a Christmas Eve party in the Grand Ballroom. But poor Lord Candy has collapsed! "Mr X poisoned my Christmas candies, then stole my keys to the Maze Cube!" he gasps. "And he left you a maze puzzle to keep you dancing around the Ballroom floor. There's no way to stop him now!"

The other detectives look as if they have given up hope. But the Maze Detective knows there is always a way! First things first: before the keys, you must find the antidote, a small purple bottle marked with a skull and crossbones.

Bingo Caller's Request

I have lost my number 6! If you can find it and give it to the player who needs it, you will get half the prize.

Missing Maze Dog

Mazey the Maze Dog is the only detective fast enough to catch Mr X now! But you've lost her in the confusion. You must track Mazey down if you're to save the Maze Cube.

Mr X's Key Challenge

Dear Pierre,
The Maze Cube is almost in my grasp. I have Lord Candy's keys to its four locks, and a hot-air balloon waiting to carry it away. Your only hope is to track down the four spare keys lost in the Ballroom. I bet you can't find them in time to unlock this mystery!

From X

Confrontation at the Top

At the top of the stairs, the door opens and . . . Whoa! You are standing on the edge of the roof!

The people below are the size of ants. Snow is falling, hot-air balloons drift by, and the Maze Cube bathes everything in its golden light. Mazey has dashed ahead and is hanging on to Mr X's cloak to slow him down. It is nearly midnight and there is one final maze to solve. Quickly! Find your way to the top. You must get to the Maze Cube first . . .

Hidden Items

- ☆ 5 GOLD STARS
- 🏆 5 RED TROPHIES
- 📦 5 GREEN TREASURE CHESTS
- 📦 1 BLUE TREASURE CHEST

Secret Agent's Offer

You saved me in the Boiler Room!

Now I'm wearing a blue-and-white shirt to show I'm on your side.

Find me, and I will fight off all the other henchmen.

Request from the Pilot

I can't fly my plane in this snow, so I want to borrow a hot-air balloon. Show me the way from my green plane to the balloon launch pad, so that I can get the detectives home in time for Christmas.

Santa sighted over New Maze City

Young maze adventurer Carmen has sent us an amazing Christmas message. She claims to have seen Santa and his sleigh from the roof of New Maze Tower. Can anyone confirm her report?

The New Maze Times

Mr X the Phantom Thief Arrested
Maze Dog Saves the Day

Maze Cube saved as midnight chimes
Terrifying chase on Empire Maze Tower roof

Yesterday a letter was received by Lord Candy, owner of Empire Maze Tower. It was sent by Mr X the Phantom Thief, revealing his fiendish plot to steal the Maze Cube and force Christmas to be cancelled in New Maze City. Mr X was foiled only after many of the world's greatest detectives gave chase. Pierre the Maze Detective finally captured him, after an act of great bravery by his friend Carmen's dog, Mazey. Mr X is now said to be planning an escape from New Maze City Prison. But Pierre has promised he will have no hiding place. Pierre will find him wherever he goes. He is, after all, the Maze Detective.

MAZE DOG TO RECEIVE GOLD BONE AS REWARD
Shock as bone goes missing from millionaire's bedside

As a reward for her dogged pursuit of Mr X, Lord Candy has offered Mazey the Maze Dog a kennel in his Dream Hotel and a bone of solid gold. However, he has had to offer a second reward after the gold bone went missing. "I left it in my Grand Ballroom!" said Candy. "I call upon maze detectives everywhere to locate it."

Message to readers! Is there anything you have missed? Additional information now available!

Monster known as "Yellow Foot" reported in New Maze City

There have been a number of reported sightings of Yellow Foot on Central Street in New Maze City. Please confirm this with your own eyes.

Artist's self-portrait unveiled

Hirofumi Kamigaki, the illustrator of this book, is exhibiting a self-portrait from his student days at the Great Exhibition. Critics have had a lot to say about the picture. Why not find it and judge for yourself?

Maze Detective Challenge
Track down "P" for Pierre

To celebrate his adventure, Pierre has hidden his famous letter "P" badge in every scene of the story. Come on detectives! Find them!

Missing!
Circus acrobats lose tiger in Empire Maze Tower

One of three tigers owned by the tower's famous acrobats has been reported lost. If you spot it, please inform the acrobats' leader, who is waiting in the lobby.

QUICK QUIZ TIME

Q1. From the ship, which animal can you see that is longer than a dolphin?

Q2. What time did they arrive at the port?

Q3. What is the 3-digit number in the pink building of New Maze City?

Q4. How many people are playing the trumpet in the hotel lobby?

Q5. What animal is rampaging in the circus staff hotel room?

Q6. What other words are hidden in the library?

Q7. How many people are in the prison at the Great Exhibition?

Q8. What animals are on the stage of the Opera, other than the dragon?

Q9. What words are written in red letters on a pipe at the right side of the boiler room? (read backwards)

Q10. What is the cowboy drinking in the Grand Ballroom?

Answers: 1.Killer whale 2.12:10 3.082 4.10 5.Gorilla 6.SECRET, LIBRARY, BOOK 7.3 8.Elephant, Dog, Cat, Rat 9.THANK YOU 10.Milk

The New Maze Times

CORRECT MAZE COURSES REVEALED!
Did you find your way to the top of the tower?

— Maze
✗ Mr X's Challenge, Articles, etc.
○ Hidden Items
○ Other Items
○ Additional Maze Information, Quick Quiz Time, etc.

Detectives of all abilities played a part in capturing Mr X and ensuring the Maze Cube continues to shine its light on New Maze City. Were you one of them? Reports are in that some routes were tricky, others were fiendish, and a few made people dizzy. Pierre's routes and hidden objects are shown below. Remember, there are many ways through a maze but every maze is amazing.

On Deck

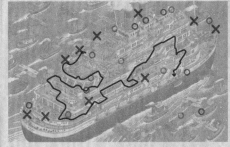
The Ocean Liner

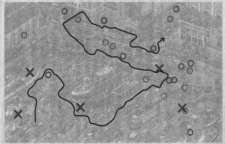
A Crowded Port

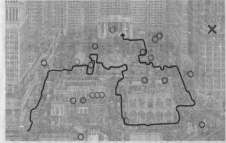
New Maze City

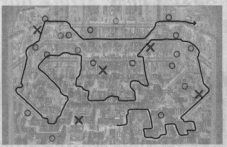
Main Lobby

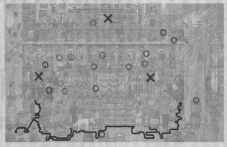
Candy Store Puzzle

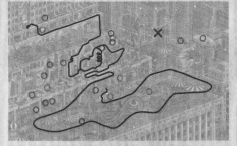
The Amusement Park

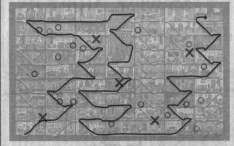
Guest Rooms

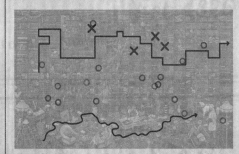
Library Puzzle

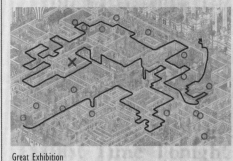
Great Exhibition

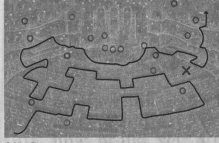
Golden Theater

Boiler Room

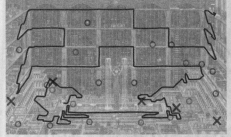
Observation Deck

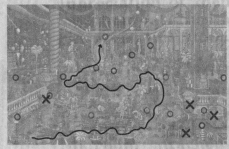
Grand Ballroom Puzzle

Confrontation at the Top

Pierre
THE MAZE DETECTIVE

SPECIAL THANKS TO

IC4DESIGN

Daisuke Matsubara

Yoko Sugi

Arisa Imamura

Masami Tatsugawa

Keiko Kamigaki

Emma Sakamiya • Naomi Leeman

Philip Contos • Alexandre Coco • Jason Hook

Andrej Schachtschneider • Agnes Kato

Benjamin LeMar • Mikiko Matsubara

Anthony-Cédric Vuagniaux • Elizabeth Jenner

Junichi Nagaoka • Yukihiko Yoshida

Leah Willey • Liza Wilde • Ella Tomkins

Isobel Doster • Milly Chapple • Sadie Smith

Kate Newport • Paula Burgess • Lucy Twist

LAURENCE KING

LAURENCE KING
This edition published in 2023 by Laurence King

First published in the United States in 2017
by Laurence King

Text and illustrations copyright © IC4DESIGN 2017

All rights reserved.

ISBN 978-1-510-23053-8

10 9 8 7 6 5 4 3 2 1

Printed in China

MIX
Paper from
responsible sources
FSC® C104740

Laurence King
An imprint of
Hachette Children's Group
Part of Hodder and Stoughton
Carmelite House
50 Victoria Embankment
London EC4Y 0DZ

An Hachette UK Company
www.hachette.co.uk
www.hachettechildrens.co.uk
www.laurenceking.com